The
Beagle

by William R. Sanford
and Carl R. Green

Edited by Julie Bach

CRESTWOOD HOUSE

New York
Collier Macmillan Canada
Toronto
Maxwell Macmillan International Publishing Group
New York   Oxford   Singapore   Sydney

Library of Congress Cataloging-in-Publication Data

Sanford, William R. (William Reynolds), 1927-
    The beagle / by William R. Sanford and Carl R. Green ; edited by Julie Bach.
  —1st ed.
        p.   cm. — (Top dog series)
    Summary: Discusses the history, physical characteristics, care, and breeding of the
  beagle.
    ISBN 0-89686-529-0
    1. Beagles (Dogs)—Juvenile literature.   [1. Beagles (Dogs)   2. Dogs.]
  I. Green, Carl R.   II. Bach, Julie S., 1963-   III. Title.   IV. Series: Top dog
  (Crestwood House)
  SF429.B3S26   1990
  636.7'53—dc20   90-34211
                                                                            CIP
                                                                             AC

PHOTO CREDITS

Cover: Animals Animals: (Robert Pearcy)
Animals Animals: (Robert Pearcy) 4;
   (Ralph A. Reinhold) 9
Judy Formisano: 6, 15, 29
Linda Forrest: 11, 12, 18, 20, 22, 25, 26, 30, 32, 35, 36, 38
Ashbey Photography: (Dave Ashbey) 41
Walter Chandoha: 42

Copyright © 1990 by Crestwood House, Macmillan Publishing Company

CRESTWOOD HOUSE

Macmillan Publishing Company
866 Third Avenue
New York, NY 10022

Collier Macmillan Canada, Inc.
1200 Eglinton Avenue East
Suite 200
Don Mills, Ontario M3C 3N1

Printed in the United States of America

First Edition

10   9   8   7   6   5   4   3   2   1

◼CONTENTS

For more information about beagles, write to:

National Beagle Club
  of America Institute Farm
Aldie, VA 22001

CHASING THE SNOWSHOE HARE

The pack of small hounds was plowing across the soft snow of the Maine countryside. Their melodic *baying* told their owner that his beagles were tracking a snow hare.

The swift hare twisted past a snowdrift and hid under a thicket. Crouching there, the frightened hare was almost invisible. The beagles overran the hare's tracks and milled about, searching for the new line.

The snow hare was a fair match for these eager hunting dogs. Its gray-brown summer coat had turned white with the coming of winter. Long hairs grew between its toes and along the sides of its feet. These "snowshoes" allowed the hare to skim lightly over the newly fallen snow.

One of the beagles picked up the scent and gave a deep baying call. The pack joined the leader and plunged into the snowdrift. Snow flew in all directions as their legs churned. The hare saw them coming and sprang out of its hiding place. The chase was on again.

The beagle is a lively, intelligent dog prized by hunters for its ability to track game over long distances.

5

One of the beagles left the pack and cut around a birch tree. The move picked up a precious ten yards on the fleeing hare. Trailing on his snowshoes, the dogs' owner shook his head and smiled. Only one dog in a thousand could outguess a hare like that. It wasn't human thinking, he knew. It was the result of centuries of careful *breeding*.

The beagles picked up speed on a patch of rocky ground. The lead dog was snapping at the hare's heels. With a last burst of speed, the hare turned and squeezed through a hole in a

These sportsmen proudly display their dogs after a field trial.

high stone wall. The pack pulled up in front of the wall, barking angrily. Seconds later, the hare was far away.

The owner called in his dogs and praised them for their fine work. He didn't mind losing the hare. The joy of the hunt lay in watching the courage and stamina of his beagles.

THE ORIGINS OF THE BEAGLE

All dogs belong to the same species, *Canis familiaris*, the domestic dog. They are meat-eating mammals, or *carnivores*, and are closely related to wolves and foxes.

Scientists think the dog was probably the first animal tamed by humans. By carefully breeding them over the centuries, people produced dogs of many sizes and shapes. One of the favorites was the *hound*, a hunting dog that tracked its prey by scent. The oldest and smallest member of the family was the beagle. Its name probably comes from the French *beigle*, meaning "small."

The beagle's ancestors first appeared in ancient Greece. Later, they traveled to Britain with the Romans around A.D. 200. The hounds stayed in Britain when the Roman armies left several centuries later. In the 10th century, King Canute banned large hounds from his royal forests. However, he did not ban the small, long-eared hounds that were forerunners of the beagle. Canute decided that these dogs were too small to harm his deer.

William the Conqueror introduced the *Talbot hound* to Britain in the 11th century. This large white hound was crossed with the smaller British hounds. Further crossbreeding produced the modern beagle, whose name first appeared in print in the 15th century. These sturdy, hard-working "hare" hounds quickly became royal favorites. One poet used these words to describe the beagle's joy in the chase:

On the wings of the wind
The merry beagles fly.

In the late 1800s, breeders produced a number of small beagles. Some of these "pocket beagles" were tiny enough to be carried home in a hunter's jacket pocket. Beagles of all sizes were prized for their musical voices and keen noses. They could follow a rabbit's scent through the thickest of underbrush. These traits also made beagles good trackers for fox hunting.

After the Civil War, beagles became favorites with hunters and their popularity spread quickly.

Americans knew little about the beagle before the Civil War. Most American hunting hounds were white dogs with a few dark markings. Old records show that they had straight, short legs and dachshundlike heads. After the Civil War, well-to-do hunters began to import British beagles. The handsome dogs caught on quickly, and the breed was recognized in America in 1885. In the 1890s, beagle fanciers, often known as *beaglers*, organized the first *field trials* and beagle clubs.

Today, the beagle ranks in the Top Ten of American breeds. Many beagles are still used

9

as hunting dogs, but most are sold as pets. Many of them are named Snoopy as a tribute to the beagle in the Peanuts comic strip. A real beagle doesn't look much like the simply drawn Snoopy, however.

THE BEAGLE IN CLOSE-UP

Beagles project strength and vitality. Their compact, well-muscled bodies mark them as working dogs. A small female may weigh as little as 20 pounds, but a large male can weigh 35 pounds.

From chest to rump, a beagle measures about 10 to 15 inches. The upright tail adds another 7 inches. A typical beagle stands 10 to 15 inches high at the *withers*. In order to qualify for American Kennel Club (AKC) competition, a beagle must not exceed 15 inches in height.

Most beagles have coats of black, tan, and white, although some are only tan and white. The white hair usually appears on the underside of the body, on the *muzzle*, and at the tip of the tail. Black and tan markings on the head

The beagle's muscular body and sleek coat give it an athletic look.

add to the dog's alert good looks. The flat coat is short, straight, and thick. Because beagles don't have undercoats, their owners brush them once a week to keep them from *shedding* too much.

If the beagle is going to be shown, the head should be of medium length and neither too long nor too round. Each floppy ear should almost reach the dog's nose if pulled forward. The ears hang at a slight forward angle over the cheeks, framing brown or hazel eyes. The nose is either black or liver colored.

Most beagles are black, tan, and white like the one shown here.

The beagle's teeth are those of a carnivore. The baby teeth fall out in the fifth month, leaving room for 42 adult teeth. The upper jaw has 6 *incisors* for cutting and 2 *canines* for ripping. Behind these front teeth are 12 *molars* and *premolars* for chewing and grinding. The lower jaw contains 2 extra molars. If properly fed, beagles seldom develop cavities.

The dog eats a bone by tearing off big chunks of meat with its incisors and canines. As soon as a bite is small enough to swallow, down it goes. When the dog is ready to gnaw the bone, it turns its head to the side and uses its molars. In the stomach, strong acids turn fats and protein into energy. In the intestines, liver bile is important in digesting fat. Fats make up 20 percent of a typical beagle's diet.

You can tell that a beagle is strong just by looking at it. The neck is long and powerful; the back is short and straight. Owners never *dock*, or shorten, the tail, which most beagles carry high and erect. The forelegs are straight, with the upper joint, the elbow, held close to the body. The wide, muscular hindquarters are set with the feet pointing directly forward. This compact form gives the beagle speed and endurance to chase rabbits.

If you watch a beagle in action, you'll see that it has three *gaits*. When it's walking slowly, one foot at a time leaves the ground. When its head is down in a trot, the right-front and left-rear legs move together. In the next instant, the left-front and right-rear legs swing forward to complete the cycle. In a full-speed gallop, the dog springs forward off its hind legs. When the forelegs hit, it bounds forward again. With this motion, a beagle can cover a lot of ground in a hurry.

THE BEAGLE'S SENSES

Not long ago, a three-year-old boy wandered away from his family's farm, followed by the family's two beagles. When the boy became lost in the woods and the temperature fell to freezing, the beagles curled up against the child and kept him warm. His father found him the next day, hungry but unhurt.

Were the beagles displaying intelligence when they stayed with the toddler? Scientists would say the dogs were operating on *instinct*, not intelligence. Intelligence is related to brain

A keen sense of smell allows beagles to find game and even people who are lost in the woods.

size, they say. Humans, with their three-pound brains, are the most intelligent animals on earth. Dogs, with their two-and-a-half-ounce brains, are not quite as smart.

Here's an experiment you can do to see how a dog's instincts work: Hide one of your dog's favorite toys under a bush. Then turn your dog loose to sniff it out. Repeat the game several times, always hiding the toy in the same place. When the dog has learned the game, change the rules. Hide the toy in a new place. Your dog will rush to the old hiding place. When it can't find the toy, it will bark excitedly and paw at the ground, certain that the toy must be there.

Dogs' senses are also much different from humans' senses. Beagles are color-blind, for example, but they see a wider field of vision than humans do. They also have better night vision. While they don't see well at a distance, they're more sensitive to faraway movements than humans are. Except for an extra protective eyelid called the *haw*, a beagle's eyes are similar to your own. Indeed, it's not unusual for beagles to be nearsighted.

Although a dog's eyes aren't very sharp, its ears are incredibly keen. A beagle can hear higher tones and detect fainter sounds than any human can. Blow on a "silent" dog whistle and your dog will come running. You can't hear its high tones, but a beagle can. A beagle can also hear the faint rustle of a cottontail creeping through the grass. It'll be off and running while you're wondering what's happening.

A beagle's sense of smell is even better than its sense of hearing. The odor-sensing nerve endings in the human nose are tiny compared to those in a beagle's moist black nose. Every breath the dog takes opens up a world of scent that humans can't begin to imagine. A rabbit, for example, leaves only the tiniest traces of scent behind as it flees through the woods. To a beagle, the path of smells is as easy to follow as a well-lighted road.

With this sense of smell, a beagle can pick its owner out of a crowd by sniffing out his or her body scent. After you touch a dog dish, a beagle can pick that dish out of a hundred similar dishes. Odors can also cause emotional reactions in dogs. A whiff of fresh meat will send a beagle into a joyous dance. But the scent of fear on a stranger will cause it to snarl and bare its teeth.

A DOG WITH CHARACTER

The crisp fall day is perfect for a ramble through the woods. A young woman walks along a muddy path with her beagle. With its nose alert to each new scent, the dog sniffs at every grass clump and bramble thicket. It strikes a rabbit trail, and its melodious bark breaks the silence. "Heel, Buddy! No rabbits today!" the woman says sharply. Instantly, the beagle will return to her side.

This brief picture gives you a good idea of the beagle's character. As much as it loves to hunt, a well-trained dog will give up the chase on command. Above all, these willing, friendly dogs want to please. Unlike more nervous breeds, they're easy to handle in public. Even when a stranger approaches, one word from its owner will calm a beagle down.

Beagles are playful dogs that enjoy being outdoors.

Beagles have been used to hunt animals as varied as rabbits, foxes, pheasants, and small kangaroos. One beagle learned to catch fish by diving off a dock on a Michigan lake. When trained for the hunt, beagles are tireless trackers. And hunters agree that their musical voices are the sweetest of all the hounds.

For every beagle trained to hunt, ten others are happy to be family pets. As pets, beagles tend to love everyone in their human families. If you go away on a long trip, your beagle will rejoice upon your return. Despite their devotion, however, they don't grieve when separated from their owners. An older beagle adopted by a new family soon adjusts to its new home. This gentle nature has made the breed a favorite research animal. Scientists have used beagles to test everything from new dog foods to the effects of air pollution.

Dog experts say it's easy to admire beagles. They make good watchdogs, but they're not vicious. When danger threatens, their loud baying wakes even the soundest sleeper. They enjoy rough play; they'll even endure a baby's pushing and pulling without complaint. Their short coats make them easy to keep clean, and they are almost never sick. What is more, beagles usually live for 14 years or more.

For all their good qualities, beagles aren't for everyone, however. Shut up all day in an apartment, a bored beagle can get into a great deal of mischief. These dogs need both exercise and attention. They thrive on daily walks and games of run and fetch.

Beagles are alert watchdogs and affectionate pets.

CHOOSING A BEAGLE PUPPY

Owning a beagle—or any dog—is serious business. Before you go puppy shopping, ask yourself some important questions.

Is it better to buy from a breeder or a pet store? Choosing a healthy, well-bred dog is the most important concern, whether you buy from a breeder or a pet store. But because puppies grow up to be like their parents, it helps to see the "adult model." This can only be done when you buy from a breeder. Also, a breeder may have several *litters* to show. A pet store often has only a single puppy for sale. You can ask a *veterinarian* for the address of a good breeder, or you can look one up in *Dog World* magazine.

How do I know the puppy is healthy? Healthy puppies are alert, playful, and clean. They shouldn't be too aggressive or too shy. Never buy a puppy that has cloudy eyes, a swollen belly, or a runny nose. Also, don't buy a puppy that doesn't hear well. You can test a puppy's hearing by snapping your fingers behind its head to see if it responds. Also, ask the seller

21

When choosing a beagle puppy, look for one that is playful and alert.

for the puppy's health record and take it to the vet for a checkup as soon as possible.

Should I buy a show dog or a pet? A show-quality dog costs about $600. A pet-quality beagle costs about $400. The extra money pays for tiny differences that only breeders and dog-show judges can see. Any well-bred beagle will have the breed's desirable character.

Is it important to buy a purebred? A *pure-bred* can be counted on to have all the qualities of the breed. A *crossbreed* puppy can turn out to look and act like a beagle—or like an entirely different dog. A breeder will have the *pedigree* for each of his or her purebred puppies. These papers list the puppy's ancestors. Register the puppy by sending the papers to one of the national kennel clubs.

Should I buy a male or a female puppy? Male or female beagles make equally good pets, show dogs, and hunting dogs. If you plan to raise puppies, you'll want to buy a female. A male puppy usually costs a little less but is more likely to roam. A female, on the other hand, comes into *heat* twice a year. This is the time she's ready to mate and have puppies. Male dogs from miles around will be attracted to her.

Of course, you don't have to breed your female beagle. Your veterinarian can *spay* her. This simple operation prevents your dog from ever getting pregnant. It costs about $100. You can also make sure your male dog doesn't make another dog pregnant. Your vet can *neuter* him. That operation costs about the same as spaying.

How old should a puppy be when it is taken home? A new puppy should be at least seven weeks old when taken from its mother.

Younger puppies need their mothers and the company of their littermates. If you don't want the task of training a puppy, look for an older dog.

TRAINING A BEAGLE PUPPY

Many trainers keep puppies in playpens when they are *housebreaking* them. The playpen keeps the puppies confined when no one is with them. They won't want to soil their sleeping places, so they'll wait to relieve themselves until the trainer takes them to a chosen place.

A puppy will usually relieve itself after it eats or when it wakes up from a nap. That's the time it should be taken to the place you want it to use. Do this every time. The odors it leaves there will encourage it to use that place again.

When a dog has an accident, be firm with it. Say "No!" in a sharp tone of voice and show it the mess. Then take the dog outside to the right spot. Afterward, scrub the soiled place to remove any odor that might tempt the dog to use it again. When the animal does perform

24   *Beagle puppies learn quickly and are easily trained.*

When training your beagle to walk on a leash, it is best to use a loose choke chain like the one shown here.

correctly, give it plenty of praise. Say "Good dog!" and pet it. A dog wants approval and will work hard to earn it.

You can train a dog to do many things. Use the same tools you used to housebreak it: patience, firmness, repetition, and reward. When the dog obeys an order, praise it and give it a bit of dog biscuit. That's called *reinforcing* the behavior. If you train the dog when it is hungry, it will work even harder to earn the treat.

When your dog is about 12 weeks old, it will

be ready for walks. Put it on a *choke chain* with thick links. At first it will try to run away as soon as you step outside. Those outdoor scents are so exciting! When it tries, pull back quickly on the chain. Say "Stay!" and loosen the chain as soon as the dog stops pulling against it. Then start off at a steady pace, dragging the dog with you until it gets the idea. Praise it when it stays by your side. Two weeks on the choke chain will turn your dog into a well-behaved companion.

To train a dog to stop chewing the furniture, catch it in the act and swat the floor with a newspaper as you scold it. But don't expect it to learn good behavior right away. Training takes time.

Every time your dog learns a command, it will find it easier to learn new ones.

◤LOVING CARE

Living with a beagle will add joy to your life. It will also add to your work load. A loving owner knows that proper care means more than feeding and housing the dog. It also means *grooming* it, taking it to a vet, and exercising it.

Like humans, beagles need balanced diets. The easiest way to feed a new puppy is to buy a high-quality packaged puppy meal. Some owners prefer to mix their own puppy foods using recipes found in dog care books. Either way, specialists recommend adding some vitamin and mineral drops.

A puppy requires small meals at least five times a day. Give it about one-half ounce of food for each pound of body weight. By nine months, the growing puppy will do nicely on two meals a day. Adult dogs need only a single evening meal plus a few dog biscuits each morning. Keep a dish of fresh water within easy reach.

What you shouldn't feed your beagle is just as important. Never give it fish or chicken bones that can splinter and stick in its throat. Your beagle will beg for sweets, but sugary foods have little food value. They can also cause cavities.

Despite their short coats, beagles can adjust to almost any climate. They can live outdoors or indoors. An indoor dog needs only a good-sized box or basket to sleep in. Line it with newspapers and an old blanket. Outdoor dogs need shelter from wind and rain. A doghouse should be large enough to allow the dog to stretch out on a raised sleeping platform.

Sleeping on the cold, damp ground can ruin a dog's health.

Grooming twice a week will keep your beagle's coat sleek and clean. Brushing smooths the coat and tones the skin. Beagles need bathing only when they've rolled in mud or filth. Use a dog shampoo, rinse thoroughly, and dry with a fluffy towel. A wet dog will always shake itself, so wear old clothes at bath time.

Beagles are healthy animals, but they do need some basic medical care. Young beagles must

Beagle puppies grow rapidly and will eat at least five times a day.

An outdoor kennel like this one is a good place for young dogs to get exercise and keep out of trouble.

have a series of puppy shots to prevent distemper and other diseases. Shampoos, flea powders, and flea collars take care of most insect pests. If a beagle develops a potbelly, runny eyes, and vomits its food, it may have *worms*. Take it to a vet at once: Worming a dog is a job for an expert.

Finally, a beagle needs an outlet for its boundless energy. A fast daily walk plus a game of Frisbee will keep both of you in good spirits. An occasional ramble in the woods will let your beagle show off its hunting skills.

BREEDING YOUR BEAGLE

Almost everyone who owns a female beagle, or *bitch*, thinks about breeding her. Breeding a beagle isn't a simple matter, however. First, consider the dog's age and health. A four-year-old is usually considered too old for a first litter. If she's going into heat for the first time, she's too young. You should generally wait for your dog's second or third heat to make sure she's in tip-top shape. Most importantly, never breed a bad-tempered dog or one that was born with a defect. Puppies are as likely to inherit bad qualities as they are good ones.

Next, you will have to find a *stud*. Most beagle kennels have a champion male reserved for breeding. It is best to visit the kennel to make sure the male is healthy. Some stud services will want to check your female, as well. A careful breeder wants all puppies to be as perfect as possible.

Once the stud is chosen, the female is taken to the stud service between the eleventh and fifteenth days of her next heat. If all goes well, she'll become pregnant after the first mating. If not, the stud's owner lets you bring the female back for a second try. You can pay the stud fee in cash or by giving the stud owner "pick of the litter." That means the owner gets to keep your female's best puppy. Some stud owners also ask for "first refusal." This gives them the right to buy one of the puppies.

Mating your dog is only the first step. Because she will still be in heat, she will have to be kept away from other males. Many breeders use "no-mate" tablets to keep pregnant females

When breeding a beagle, you must make sure that both parents are healthy and have good tempers.

safe. They also use this time to take their dogs to a vet. The vet will examine the dog and prescribe a high-protein, low-starch diet. The dog will need plenty of gentle exercise, but jumping will have to be kept to a minimum.

Your dog's pregnancy will last about 63 days. When she's almost ready to deliver, make up a *whelping box.* If the birth is normal, the dog will take care of everything else.

A LITTER OF PUPPIES

Nothing is more exciting than the birth of a new litter. Each whelping is a miracle of birth.

When your beagle is ready to deliver her puppies, she'll scratch around in the whelping box. She may pant and tremble, but this is normal. The first puppy will be born soon after the contractions begin. If the contractions go on and on without results, call a vet.

Each newborn puppy emerges head first in a birth sac. The mother tears off the sac and licks the whelp until it starts to breathe. Then she bites through the *umbilical cord,* and she may eat the afterbirth. Finally, she licks the squirming pup to clean and comfort it.

Your dog will deliver about five or six deaf, blind, and helpless puppies. A new whelp arrives every 30 minutes or so. When all of them are born, the mother nudges the whelps toward her *teats* to begin feeding. After an hour or so, separate her from the nursing puppies and take her for an easy run. Also, give her a drink of water and a dish of dog meal soaked in milk.

When the puppies are three days old, call in a vet to check them. The doctor usually removes their *dewclaws* at this time, too. Two weeks later, clip their sharp nails so they won't scratch their mother while they're nursing. Now you can begin *weaning* them. Let the puppies suck a milk-and-broth mixture from your finger. Soon they can begin lapping milk from a pan.

Beagle puppies grow fast. At three weeks their eyes open, and they can hear. Fat and awkward, tails wagging, they scramble around on unsteady legs. You'll hear them bark when they're hungry and squeal when they're frightened.

By four weeks, the puppies start to eat four or five small meals a day from a bowl. They cut their baby teeth and can chew soft

After giving birth, a beagle mother washes her puppies before nursing them.

puppy food. Their mother lets them nurse only at night. By six weeks, most beagles are completely weaned.

By the eighth week, look for homes for these healthy puppies. If you're lucky, you'll find buyers who will pay good prices for your beagles. When you subtract all your expenses, however, you may be lucky to break even. That's the breeding business. Most breeders don't do it for the money. They do it because they love beagles.

WHY DOES A BEAGLE CHASE ITS TAIL?

A healthy beagle carries its strong, white-tipped tail like a banner. Show beagles are trained to hold their tails upright in the ring. Hunting dogs often run with their tails streaming behind them. Their tails act as rudders that keep the dogs balanced when they turn sharply.

Beagle puppies often seem surprised that they have tails. What is that odd thing that follows me about? the puppy seems to say. Then it chases its tail in a wild circle. This lively chase often continues until the puppy loses interest. Some puppies spin around so many times they become dizzy.

The sight of a beagle chasing its tail is amusing. The high-spirited dog looks like it is having fun. But what if a puppy chases its tail all the time? Is its behavior natural or unhealthy?

Beagles are curious dogs that like to explore everywhere. This dog watches its reflection in a pond.

Dog experts say that the answer begins with an understanding of dog behavior. They point out that puppies are usually raised in the rough-and-tumble company of their littermates. When they're separated from the other puppies, they have no one to romp with. If a puppy's new owners leave it alone every day, the puppy may become bored. That's when serious tail-chasing can begin. The puppy's tail takes the place of missing playmates.

Most puppies outgrow this stage. If they don't stop, it's a sign that they need more

Beagles need simple toys, like this bone, to play with when they're left alone.

stimulation. Dogs that don't get enough exercise and attention can have other behavior problems as well. A beagle may bite its paws, pace back and forth, or whine constantly. Some dogs bite themselves hard enough to cause ugly sores.

An older dog may suddenly start chasing its tail for a medical reason. The dog may have developed swollen anal glands or a skin infection. A vet can diagnose and treat these conditions.

It's up to the dog's owner to treat a case of boredom. Dogs need an assortment of toys to play with when they're left alone. Rawhide bones, balls, and other simple toys usually do the trick. Daily play and exercise are also vital to a beagle's emotional health. There isn't a beagle alive who would rather chase its tail than chase a rabbit or a stick.

BEAGLE CHAMPIONSHIPS

It happens to all beaglers at one time or another. You visit a dog show and before long you are thinking, My dog could win this show!

Or you visit a *field trial* to watch beagles tracking wild rabbits. This time you think, My beagle has a better nose than any of those dogs.

Perhaps your dog is a super beagle. But it will never win a show or a trial if it's not properly prepared. Silver cups and blue ribbons don't happen by accident. It takes a good pedigree and long hours of training to get a dog ready for competition.

A dog show is primarily a "beauty contest." A dog can win only if it meets the standards set for its breed. Owners usually ask breeders or people who show beagles to look at their dogs before entering them in any competition. If they say the dogs are show-quality, it's time to begin training.

The judges expect every dog to control its usual high spirits while it's in the ring. You'll need to train your dog to heel perfectly and to stand quietly. It'll have to ignore other dogs and allow strangers to poke and pull at it. Practice all this at home until the dog performs perfectly. Then try competing in a puppy class or a novice class. If your dog does well there, you can move up to stiffer competition.

Because beagles were first bred as hunting dogs, some owners prefer to compete in field

Long hours of obedience training and grooming paid off for this handsome beagle, which will go home with a blue ribbon.

trials. Field trial judges don't worry about a dog's looks. They are more interested in how well it tracks rabbits. Your job will be to direct your beagle's natural hunting instincts to that task.

To begin, take your beagle into open fields where it can learn to use its nose. If it runs off and gets lost, remain in place and call it. When your dog returns, praise it. This encourages the dog to become expert at following its own trail back to you.

Next, beat the bushes with a stick until you scare up a rabbit. Don't worry if at first your dog doesn't know what to do. Encourage it to sniff the trail. After a number of rabbits are flushed, your dog will get the idea. With praise ringing in its ears, your beagle will gallop after the elusive cottontail.

All this is only a start, of course. Your beagle still has many lessons to learn. But if it has a stout heart and you have plenty of patience to train it, your dog may become a field trial champion.

COTTONTAIL TRIALS

A century ago the National Beagle Club held the first cottontail field trial in Hyannis, Massachusetts. Today, more than 400 official trials are held in this country. Some trials attract as many as 200 beagles and their handlers.

Each club works hard to keep its running grounds stocked with rabbits. The members plant food crops for rabbits, and during harsh winters they scatter extra food around

With good training, beagles can become excellent hunting companions.

the grounds. A kennel and clubhouse provide shelter for dogs and members during stormy weather.

On the day of the trial, the owner fills out an entry form. The form asks for such items as the dog's name, the class it will run in, and the name of its handler. The beagles are divided into two classes. One class is for dogs under 13 inches. The other is for dogs 13 to 15 inches. Beagles who measure over 15 inches are not allowed to run.

In the most common kind of trial, the judges divide the beagles into *braces*, or pairs. Females run against females and males against males. Other trials send the dogs out in *packs* of varying sizes. A small pack is made up of four to seven dogs. A large pack often includes all of the dogs entered in a class.

The trial begins when "beaters" move out to beat the bushes. As soon as a rabbit breaks from cover, the cry of "Tallyho!" rings out. The handlers send their two beagles in pursuit. Then they follow the brace, shouting commands for changes in direction. If a second rabbit breaks cover, both dogs are called back. The handlers then restart them on the line of the first cottontail.

Two judges on horseback grade the beagles. The judges give more points for a dog's skill in following the scent than for sheer speed. They also award high marks for giving voice while on the scent, for obedience and for endurance. The judges watch most carefully when the rabbit makes a sharp turn that causes the beagles to overrun the scent. A well-trained dog turns quickly and circles back to pick up the scent again. Poorly trained dogs wander around, unsure of what to do next. A talented beagle will rediscover the scent and spring off on the new line, giving voice as it runs.

At the end of a run, or heat, the judge gives each beagle a score. Winners go on to a second heat and possibly a third. Since beagles were once pack animals, some trials send the first-round winners out in a pack for the second run. Afterward, the judges name the first, second, third, fourth, and reserve winners. A beagle that chalks up 120 points (including three first places) earns the title of Field Champion. Proud owners say that is one of the rewards of owning a spirited and loyal beagle.

GLOSSARY/INDEX

Baying 5—The deep, prolonged barking of a hound.

Beaglers 9—Beagle owners or breeders.

Bitch 31—An adult female dog.

Braces 44—Pairs of beagles selected to compete against each other in field trials.

Breeding 6, 7, 31, 35—Mating a quality female to a quality male.

Canines 13—The four long, sharp holding teeth in the front of a dog's mouth.

Carnivores 7, 13—Meat-eating animals.

Choke Chain 27—A leash made from heavy metal links, which is used in training a dog.

Crossbreed 23—A dog whose parents are different breeds.

Dewclaws 34—Extra, useless claws that grow on the insides of a dog's legs. These are removed shortly after birth by a vet.

Dock 13—Shorten a dog's tail by cutting it off at the first or second joint.

Field Trial 9, 40, 41, 43, 45—A competition to show how well a dog can hunt.

Gait 14—The movements of a dog's feet when it is walking, trotting, or running.

Grooming 27, 29—Bathing and brushing a dog to keep its coat clean and smooth.

Haw 16—An extra eyelid that helps protect a dog's eye.

Heat 23, 31, 32—The days when a bitch is ready to mate.

Hound 7—A hunting dog that locates its prey by scent.

Housebreaking 24, 26—Training a puppy to relieve itself on newspaper or outside the house.

Incisors 13—The nipping and cutting teeth between the canines.

Instinct 14, 15, 41—Natural behavior that is inborn in a dog.

Litter 21, 33—A family of puppies born at a single whelping.

Molars 13—A dog's back teeth, used for chewing and grinding.

Muzzle 10—The mouth, jaws, and nose of a dog.

Neuter 23—To operate on a male dog so he can't make a female dog pregnant.

Pack 44—Group of beagles sent to hunt together.

Pedigree 23—A chart that lists a dog's ancestors.

Premolars 13—A dog's teeth located in front of the molars. They are used for chewing and grinding.

Purebred 22, 23—A dog whose ancestors were all of the same breed.

Reinforcing 26—Giving a dog a reward when it obeys a command.

Shedding 12—Losing hair.

Show Dog 22—A dog that meets the highest standards of its breed.

Spay 23—To remove a female dog's ovaries so she can't get pregnant.

Stud 31, 32—A purebred male used for breeding.

Talbot Hound 8—The large white hound that was an ancestor of the beagle.

Teats 34—A female dog's nipples. Puppies suck on the teats to get milk.

Umbilical Cord 33—A hollow tube that carries nutrients to a puppy while it is still inside its mother's body.

Veterinarian 21, 23, 30, 33, 34, 39—A doctor trained to take care of animals.

Weaning 34, 35—Making a puppy stop drinking its mother's milk and eat solid food instead.

Whelping Box 33—A box in which a female dog can give birth to her puppies.

Withers 10—A dog's shoulders; the point where its neck joins the body. A dog's height is measured at the withers.

Worms 30—Parasites that live in a dog's intestines and can make it sick.